Like Lazarus I Came Forth

Like Lazarus I Came Forth

poems

wayne powers

Writers Club Press
New York Lincoln Shanghai

Like Lazarus I Came Forth
poems

Writers Club Press
an imprint of iUniverse, Inc.

For information address:
iUniverse, Inc.
2021 Pine Lake Road, Suite 100
Lincoln, NE 68512
www.iuniverse.com

ISBN: 0-595-27071-9

Printed in the United States of America

Contents

Acknowledgments

Louis—My partner, best friend, supporter. This year has been both trying and exuberant. You have been beside me through it all, good and bad, believing and whispering encouragements. I love you. I can't believe it's been five years. Boy, time sure does fly when you're having fun. I couldn't do this without you.

Kelley—"When the student is ready the teacher will appear." You have no idea the impact you have had on my professional life as a writer. Your presence made me realize that *I* am a writer. But more than that you believed enough to give me work. I will forever praise your name.

Jeanine and Mark—I can't believe we've only known each other for a little over a year. You guys have come into our lives and have become welcomed fixtures bearing talent and a willingness to share. Jeanine, You're not only my agent and business partner, but I look to you like the sister I never had. We love you guys.

Jake and Luxe—I'm going to teach you to read one day, my little lovers.

I would also like to thank the following:

Jo and Frank, Phyllis and Alfie, Anthony, Brad, Base, Angela Bain, Mary Green, Evelyn Horne, Pat Pascal, Pia Engles (I learned the art of thinking BIG from you), Carolyn K. Raye, Laura N, Justin, Jonathan, Lee, Kimberly, Mark G, the Allebrande's, Caroline, Mom, Dad, Kevin, and all my clients from Columbia (who have followed my life for the past four years and have inadvertently made this possible), and to all my faithful clients in New York City.

Introduction

Most of the poems in this collection were written a decade ago when I first came out of the proverbial closet. I had just begun the first "open" relationship that I had had with a man.

Although he wasn't my first love (I had been in love a time before), I regarded this particular relationship with the excitement and fervor of a first love. It was magical. I couldn't breathe without thinking about him. It was a definite turning point in my life. A special time I wanted to share with the people I cared about.

The choice of coming out for me was confounded by the fact that I was very religious and very involved in Church related activities. I had grown up in the Baptist church, and it was an important part of my life.

I had for years been struggling with the fact that I was homosexual. Although I knew it to be true on an unconscious level, I lacked the courage to confess it to myself and inevitably to everyone else. At the time of this particular relationship, I was a senior at USC and within months was about to graduate.

The prior summer was spent in Alaska where I served as a missionary for the Baptist Student Union. Still struggling with the fact of my homosexuality, I thought that that summer would be the turning point I had been praying for. It would be my chance to change.

For years I had been struggling with my sexuality and if what I had been taught about homosexuality, in church, was true, then that summer would be the opportunity I needed to help in my change from gay to straight. I was going to be living hundreds of miles away from my environment, and if anyone could truly change their sexual orientation, this would be my defining moment.

I would do anything necessary as a "good Christian" to make and allow this change to occur.

While in Alaska, I was astounded by it's beauty. This vast land of fir trees and snow-topped mountains was picturesque. I descended the steps of the plane at the Juneau airport and was taken aback by the smell in the air. It was the freshest air I had ever inhaled. This would be the perfect place for a life-altering experience.

I armed myself with prayer, scripture, and a number of books that dealt with fasting. I dedicated my summer to nothing but change. A sexual overhaul. I was going to become straight!

However, it wasn't as easy as planned. I lived in the same, perpetual mental hell the entire summer, I had lived in all my life. Each time I had homosexual thoughts I was devastated. I would immediately pray for forgiveness. This was the schizophrenia I had lived with on a daily basis for the past twenty three years, literally hating myself for thoughts and feelings that seem to invade and color every aspect of my existence. This internal conflict was confounded by the fact that I would see heterosexual couples, obviously in love with one another, living a life of seemingly happiness. Somehow they were more complete. I longed for this intimacy.

At the time, I believed that that type of intimacy only existed between heterosexual couples. In the world I had lived in, homosexuals were nothing more than depraved and disgusting. This was what I had brought away from the many lessons I had learned in the Baptist church. I was envious of what I thought only straight people could have. I too wanted someone to have an honest, loving relationship with.

This was the up and down hell I had lived in, the roller coaster of homosexuality in Baptist circles.

I would have a sexual encounter with someone and hate myself for days afterward because of the guilt I was taught to swallow.

For years I had a relationship with someone, which on some level was a real, loving relationship. I loved him and I knew he loved me. However, because of where we came from (Lancaster, South Carolina), we knew we couldn't be together. Although we shared intimate moments that were just as real as anyone else's, we were destined to be only best friends. I was deeply in love with this guy, but I knew that no matter how much love we shared, our love would never be enough. For starters, I was a prominent Christian, a "good boy" preparing for the ministry. He, on the other hand, was a ladies' man; suave with mysterious dark features and the talent of touch.

My life dangled on the ledge. I just couldn't live this lie any longer. I couldn't allow my heart to be torn apart continuously. We went our separate ways. He went on to marry and have the straight life I had dreamed of.

Alaska was to be my turning point. I was coming home straight!

So, for the rest of the summer I did little else than think about change. I prayed for change. I fasted for change. Yet, when I came back to South Carolina, two months later, nothing had changed.

I felt powerless, confused and downright tired of fighting. I desperately wanted and needed to love myself and someone else.

I went back to school weeks after my return completely depleted. Once back I went straight way to having sex with a guy I was friends with. And I also went right back to the guilt and shame.

One night that fall, I was invited to see a movie at the campus theatre with a group of friends from the Baptist Student Union. It was a love story entitled *Before Sunrise.* It starred Ethan Hawke. I was completely taken with the movie. The raw emotions the characters felt toward one another was what I left longing for. I needed someone to love, and if that meant giving up this cleverly constructed world I had created, then so be it. I was willing to follow my heart. I couldn't pretend any longer. I wanted to live for me. Not for what my mother or father believes. Not even for what the church taught *me* to believe. I had to find the Truth for myself what ever that was.

I left the theatre with a prayer in my heart. I prayed to fall in love. I desired it with every inch of my being, and I knew love was on its way. It was in the air. I could hear it in the songs the birds sang.

In preparation, I started taking care of myself. I began an exercise regime and quickly lost twenty pounds I had gained from sadness. I was ready to step up to Life. I, too, must be counted. I, too, had something to say.

I started wearing contact lenses (I had worn coke bottled glasses since I was five years old) and started dressing more fashionably. A month or two later, I met the guy I would spend the next three years with.

I was in heaven. At the start of our relationship, I still was living a double life. Because South Carolina was so small, I had to sneak around just to be with him. Careful that no one would see us together. I hated that. I had always prided myself on the fact that I was an honest person, yet, on the most basic level of my life, I had been taught to lie.

I wanted to be truthful.

I came clean, and told everyone I knew that I was in love…with a man!

For the first time in my life, I understood what Jesus meant when he said "The truth will set you free." I was free. I no longer worried about being caught. I no longer fretted about secrecy and scandal.

I no longer lived one life two ways.

I was free to be the authentic me, and I didn't care what anyone else thought about it. I was the person I was meant to be. Finally, for once in my life I was happy. I knew I had come into myself. And I didn't care what anyone had to say about it either.

Once I came out, I spent many nights afraid that everyone I had known would turn their backs on me. I cried a lot during this period. Luckily, I found poetry or more appropriately poetry found me.

Poetry literally saved my life. I could put all of my feelings into words and have them dispelled before me on the page. I wrote constantly. I carried a notebook everywhere I went. I put my life to the page. Notebook after notebook, I wrote poems of love, confusion, and betrayal. Many of these poems were about my relationship with God and the church.

After months, I came to realize that God and the church were two different entities. I had tried to come to terms with my relationship with God, but I was doing it within the context of what I had been taught in church, not by what I had experienced.

But my experience was the opposite. My experience had taught me that I couldn't change. I was who I was and that was that. I had only two choices in the matter. I could be the person I was born to be, or I could live a life of unhappiness, and hide myself in twenty pounds of misery, and pray that no one ever found out about my sexual exploits.

I chose happiness.

I couldn't come to grips with the fact that God had created me to live a life of unhappiness. The Bible says that Jesus came to give Life and a Life filled with abundance, not a Life riddled with pain and painted in guilt.

When I finally came out, I told close friends of my church family not really knowing what would happen. I was praying that everyone would understand and accept me as I am. But I *was* Baptist.

At the time, I was very close to the pastor of the church I had attended since childhood. I was also a close friend of the Youth Leader. Because she and I were so close, I confided in her first. I was young and naïve and felt at the time that our relationship wouldn't be any different. I wanted her to be happy for me. I was in love. Everything in my life looked up. But after talking with her, I knew nothing would ever be the same.

When we talked months later, she confided what the pastor had said. Because I had been so involved in the ministry, essentially, he thought I had been deceitful to everyone.

At first, I was deeply hurt. Then I became angry. I wasn't the one who had lied! I had been lied to!

I had been brainwashed to believe that homosexuality was an abomination to God, and ultimately, that it *was* a choice. Homosexuality isn't like buying a car. It is your sexual orientation and identity. It isn't something you can control.

The only choice is acceptance.

After coming out, I spent years feeling paralyzed in my relationship with God because of what had happened with my church family. How dare they say I had been the liar. Of course, I had lied. They were the ones teaching me and everyone else that I *had* to lie.

I was the one lied to.

I continued to pray and God through his grace continued to answer my prayers. He never left me. I was never alone.

Yet, there were some unresolved issues about religion that I was still dealing with. I was devastated when I was rejected from my church family. And at that point in my life I hadn't fully dealt with those issues.

Then it suddenly dawned on me that God was not the church. Although the church was meant to be ambassadors for God, it wasn't infallible. The church is made up of people with faults and prejudice. After this revelation, I was able to put everything behind me. I still love those people, faults and all. But now, I love myself more.

It is my prayer that these poems minister to anyone dealing with homosexuality. It's still hard coming out, even in today's climate of politically correctness.

It is my intention for this book to be a vehicle of grace for anyone struggling with coming out.

God loves you. Just as you are. He's the one who molded you. He's the one who whispered in your ear as you were in your mother's womb. He knows the number of hairs on your head.

You are not doomed for "hell" just because you are gay. You are not a deviant. God does not regard you with contempt, only love. An unconditional love that never changes.

Being homosexual is a part of your being. It's your essence and you can't change your essence. And you shouldn't want to. You are special. You have a mission to accomplish on this planet. There's something for you to do that no one in history but you can do.

You came from love and you will return to love. Isn't it time that we start loving each other and ourselves?

New York City, N.Y.
January 30, 2003

These are not poetic times

"Don't you know they're talking about a Revolution? It sounds like a whisper."

—Tracy Chapman

This Is Not Poetry

In these uncertain times we clamor for Peace...wailing walls tremble earthquakes of explosions...buses and planes now weapons of mass destruction singeing hair and skin...religiously blowing away lives over pepperoni pizza and cups of fresh coffee...we take it black.

This is not Poetry

These are not Poetic times

Christ would shudder at the thought of going to work...glass and metal break and melt and while commonly used *for* you can be used against you...Towers crashing can be heard the world over like the sound of nails through bone and wood...Father, why hast thou forsaken us?

This is not Poetry

We must think and rest by the River
We must seek and not be blindly led toward destruction

Remember Hitler...while one puny man with an uneven mustache and thinning hair...too many people listened...concentrating on words as they built camps of terror and gas and dug holes big enough and deep enough and wide enough for thousands (perhaps millions) of burnt bodies...have you smelled the smell of burnt flesh?

History repeats lessons never learned:
We must listen
We must learn and think and pray and seek

We must seek Peace
at all cost
before it costs too much.

Everyday Occurrences

i

a girl at work
told me
i chose to be
Gay.
i pondered on it
& here's what i
think:
of all people,
she
being a woman
& furthermore black
should know
no one
would choose
to have a Strong Arm
held against them.

ii

it's not like
i woke up
one glorious morning
& decided this
'life style'
for myself.
i don't *even*
agree with those
words:
    LIFE
    STYLE
because I know
from the dredges of pain
the misplaced trust
the jobs i've lost or haven't gotten
& the whispers of erstwhile friends
that,
(& i'll say it only once)
it is not FASHIONABLE to be queer!

iii

we were
walking
d
o
w
n
some street
(?)
in Atlanta
holding hands
when quite suddenly
we noticed
cars screeching to sudden halts.
people staring
& whispering
& pointing at us.
Some Spectacle.
and there we were
thinking:
hadn't everyone
seen 2 men
holding hands before?

iv

i've often dreamed
a dream
in which my parents knew me,
accepted that
i liked men,
& shared in my happiness
when I found the right one.

i dreamed
of my wedding.
my father gave me away
with a smile.
my mother cried
in the pew (as all mothers do).
my brother creamed our car
'Justly Married'.

our reception was huge.
a white cake-3 tiers.
my whole family
aunts uncles 1st & 2nd cousins
laughing
over pink punch & Catalina weenies.

i woke up
reveling in this dream
watching for shooting stars
looking for four leafed clovers
& praying that dreams really do
come true.

There's Still a Revolution

you say the revolution
has ended
but it's the subtleties
we now battle
    Waging on
    War song
the slight stares
omnivorous glares
subtle gestures
your sermon's pastors
feeding from the fields of
Hate & Fear
curling upon itself
like a downward staircase
leading back into
Oblivion.
oh yes,
there's still a revolution.

I Must Remember

i must remember
the cords of chewing tobacco
and the tins of snuff
the spit tune lined
with paper towels
the rocking chair
painted every other year—
the swing and the switches

i must remember
the smell of the work shed
a mix of gasoline and oil
and metal devices used
to sharpen lawn mower blades.

i must remember
the biscuits and iced tea
the fat back and the corn bread
wrapped on the stove

i must remember
the Sundays
lazy and hot after church dinners
with ham and boiled spare ribs
and homemade apple pies

i must remember
the Cherokee
skinned woman

her white hair always set
summer gloves put away
in the cedar armoire

i must remember
the olive skinned man
overalls and hats and
Winston cigarettes
bones weary
from cotton and nine children

i must remember
the sound of the furnace
and the tick tock
of cuckoo clocks
and the creeping
of wooden floors
and the polished poster bed

i must remember
her beads and broaches
the feathers in his hat
and the pocket knife
he used to clean his nails

i must remember
because it's easy
to forget.

When You're Away

My muscles deplete
when you're away.
Tired from the
Loss
of sleep.
the
Tossing
Tossing
Turning
in sheets too
Cold
from the lack
of your
Body's Heat.

Things I Learned In Church

i learned of
Love—
as exacting as painful
always unexpected—
showed up in that Place.

his eyes
filled with specks
of brown
& the mysteries
of the Covenant.

he still
haunts me fondly
after all,
he taught me the art
of Fucking—baby oil and French kisses
in the middle of woods—
a nearby sign
Nailed
—No Trespassing—
and the secret rubbings
in the Sunday School room.

i learned of
Guilt & Shame—
the hatred for myself
growing with each
hard on.
the orgasms

overshadowed
by the luminous
shadow of the
Cross.

i learned of
Fear—
a vengeful God
keeping score
with fire &
pillars of salt
the gnashing of teeth
& brimstone.

I learned of
Betrayal &Lust—
Forgiveness & Redemption—
His Blood flowing
as freely as our
cum
the Wine as bitter
as his tongue.

The Crease in Your Brow
(for Robert Bellhue)

The crease in your brow
farmed by bitter hatred
and caustic repression
marks the resistance
of your Soul—
Staunch but shaken
Cracked not broken

You

I touch you
Blood hard against
My fingertips
I taste you
The salty smell
Cream white
Against my lips
I feel you
Painfully
Pleasurably
Inside my hips

What Makes a Man?

What makes a man a man?
The length between his legs?
The bruises on his lover?
The abundance of scars
on his face?

Or could it be the capacity for Tears,
the ability of forgiveness,
the profundity to be
Gentle?

Circa 2000

A'int nothing much changed
Maybe a few minds
Maybe a few hearts
But things pretty much the same.

People still being lynched
Blood still pouring
Tears still flowing
Riotous voices & fists still clenched.

Martyrs of their own kind
Calling out from their graves
Pleading & Praying, Weeping & Hoping
That something will force us to change.

A Revolutionary

i've been taught
never stray from the
straight & narrow
wear Predictability
        as a choker
and for God's sake
'do what's expected'

but i've learned
what maybe natural for some folk
is unnatural for me.
so i took my own path
one with briars, sharp rocks,
grown up with weeds
and let me tell you,
i knew i had stepped
from the beaten path
when the path started
beating me back.

Dear God,

the preacher said i had sinned
but i can't contain this raging
this looking, this thirst, these burning desires.
how do i control
this thing?
how can i keep my feelings at bay?
i've tried to pray it away
fast it away
baptize it away.
did you hear my supplications,
feel my hunger pangs,
know how wet I got?

Dear Child,

I made you in mine own image
watched you grow   butterfly collars & plaid suits
I was there at your Conception
What a miracle it was
The liquid lightening of
Love & Life
Converging
I was there when your mother
First held you
You were crying   cold & confused
I saw the tears in her eyes
as she promised to do right by you
I watched you grow in stature
going to church
eager to hear & learn my Word
I helped you write the songs you sang
I helped you to speak

I am the Way
I am the Truth
I am the Life

Of course I heard you pray
I knew you had hungered
I saw you baptized—
Twice
You were afraid the first one didn't take.

You are my child
I created you
I love you dearly
just as you are
nothing more, nothing less.
it just wouldn't be you
I created you to be a beacon
a Light that shines and is not afraid
one that will not hide
one that will stand and simply say,
'That I am Love not hate. That I Heal, not destroy.
That I make barren wombs full with Life.'

I am Love
I am Life
And the Creator of Love and Life.

You are not a deviant!
You are not a biological error!
You have come from Love
and Love makes no mistakes
and nothing queer!

Requiem For a Dead Saint
(for hazel lawrence powers)

i

i viewed your body and noticed
dirt was still beneath your nails
the embalming didn't even change
the hue of your skin
and those wild eyebrows
so wiry and unkempt
the ring you wore still
on your finger i couldn't pry it loose
i wanted to keep it for myself,
for your memory
a circle is forever you know
i glanced around the chilly room
after seeing you lying there so still and stiffly
and noticed the flowers.

ii

i must admit at first it startled me
maybe you could be losing your mind
senility carving away your brain
like the cancer in your lungs
partly, because only you could see them,
and partly out of disbelief—
their long white hair and shiny garments
sounded too fantastical
but with your passing i fully realized
their existence to be true
not only in your head
but on the clock.

iii

i left you at the cemetery but
even an airtight casket cannot contain you
i see you still
walking among the living
i hear your voice in the crowded world.

iv

to this day I don't believe
you were given a proper burial.
proper for a commoner
but for a Saint
some vigil was lost.

Walkin' On

Put on your walkin' shoes
Up and down the boulevard.
Your merchandise on ardent display
Before creeping, lurking cars.

Twenty dollars will do it
Your services honed to please.
Fifty dollars for the 'Super Deluxe'
Still priced way to cheap.

Walkin' on, walkin' on
'til the early dawn.
Up and down and all around
your body as your pawn.

Father, I have Sinned

innocence crucified
to rectory walls with
sucking sounds reverberating
off cathedral ceilings.
the black eyes of Jesus and Mary follow you
throughout the sanctuary.

"God will punish you if you ever tell anyone. This is part of your penance."

"father, I have sinned..."
tiny hands still wet from the clay
used to mold an imprint at school.
"I've had bad thoughts..."
his small penis pushed hard against his jeans.
at first, there's a loud pause on the other side of the confessional.

"Just give me three hail Mary's and come and sit on my lap."

he obliged.
his mother had counseled
to listen to the priest.
"He's the man of God."

"mama, father matherdi
teaches that we should love others
as ourselves. Is that why he taught me
to masturbate?"

No one wants to play soccer anymore

"But, most of all, did we write exactly what we saw, as clearly as we could? Were we unsophisticated enough to cry and scream."
"Each one, Pull one"

—Alice Walker

Louis

the night we met i was
wandering wondering
searching groping in
darkness looking for Light.

our eyes met from across
the dirtied dance floor
boas flying in the smoke filled air
feathers crashing to the floor
like the wall i had built around myself.

i came to you
and offered a drink
careful not to prematurely offer my soul
as i had become accustomed to doing.

you seemed a mystery to me
better than any Agatha Christie
deeper than perhaps
the oceans

i wasn't sure of your thoughts
were you interestingly interested
would this meeting
transpire to anything or just
evaporate like rice water?

we progressed, danced together
and Danced
the swaying of your hips
hypnotizing
taming my cobra
your eyes brown like soft leather
hands as smooth as blown glass.

we dated
goat feathers and amaretto sours
frosted flakes and 2% milk

we progressed
trying this relationship on for size.
Perfect Fit!
like a glove in a snow storm
frozen frost bitten hands
screamed Relief!

now we
Laugh together
Stay together
Hope and Pray together
Dream together
Share together
Love and Live together

We are
to gether too gether two gether

Living our daily existence of
beans and rice and merita old fashioned white bread
Planning for futures
Living for the time being
Loving in the moment
Loving living
Living loving

Heavy Love

Palamon can't boast.
His chivalrous act would
Weigh but an ounce
Compared to this
Heavy love.
How Emilye would
Faint at the measure.
The mere weight of it too great
For her shrunken shoulders.
His sword a stick beside the razor edge
Of my tongue.

Pubic Scent

The press of our skin melting.
Sticky gum pulled
Sweat off flesh
And skin.

Our thighs writhing
Rising like breakers
Bobbing wet stations
Of men.

Four arms flailing
Flying like bombers
Diving to the stress
Of sin.

Puckered lips mashing
Velvety orbs pouting
Heat and perfume
Of pubic scent.

Her Body

her body
the first I had seen
Dead.
hands stiff
fingernails velvety purple
her face a
splat
on the kitchen floor.

my grand—
father
unsteady in his
gait
bending over
her spilled ice cream
dripping chocolate
from the wooden spoon.

The Reckoning

the moon stalks
the water's surface
Uncontrolled light
swaying back and forth
on the breaking waves
like a grandmother
in a rocking chair
holding Death
in a jar.

A Dying Love

the sharpness of your
Voice
inflicts stabs to my eardrums
the Silence
between your words
speak to me of
Death.

Grave Sin
(for all Afghanistan homosexuals who have become martyrs for simply existing)

through the muffled
yells & dark overhead
silhouettes
the sun scratches at my
eyes in decisive intervals

i blink   my tear ducts
cry dust & dirt & red
clay lines my ears.

the bulldozer's engine hums
just above the mound of wet mud
earthen walls collide in
on my waist
snapping my ankles
crashing in on my ribs

i hold my breath
not wanting to breathe in
the smell of death
& immediately i think
of napalm & anthrax
& the nature of

human beings to be so
easily enticed
to the ledge of
fear.

afgan brothers slam
rocks against my face
pouring blood up my nose
as my teeth
are cracking

<Love—the hostage of talibanned hate>

through the haze i think
i hear
abdul cry for mercy
but i could be mistaken
it may be my mother
in the crowd.

no one wants to play soccer anymore

Dreadlocks

i sleep in the folds
of your hair.
oceans of curls
spread wide my legs
& open me
with the smell of almonds
and a wildness
only nature could know.
it's the mystery
that astounds me.
the kinks interlocking
like the thrashing of our bodies—
dreadlocked to eternity.

Mother,

Mother,
how I've wanted
to talk to you
to get your unadulterated
Opinion
without judgments
veiled by baptismals & Sunday School reports.

How i've wanted to
call you & really talk
like mother & son.
Things i truly
need to know—
of Love & Life
& Love…& Love…

My need to open up
to you like a canyon
show you, explain to you
make you see
the authentic me.
myself without any
apprehensions.
without any closings
that shut out the truth

like a never ending
Lie—
I don't want to lie to you
Mother.

Mother,
i want you to know me
but i've been
Afraid
Fear has taught me to
  fear myself
  be ashamed of myself
  hate myself
  hide myself
  reject myself
  repress myself
  judge myself
  psychoanalyze myself
feeding myself into
an Oblivion of
whirlwinds where
the heroine trips are
Black Beauty, &
Vicodine the evening's cocktail.

i feel i don't even know
you
Mother—
who are you?

What has caused the lines
on your rounded face?
Who has caused your hair to gray?
i want to know
how many times your heart
has been broken—
shattered like a Christmas ball
turned over & fallen.

How many boys
did you like or love
or hate or would have liked
to love to lost your virginity—
like you lost your wedding ring
in the preacher's backyard playing badminton
cursing under your breath
hoping no one would hear.

What makes you tick?
What turns you on off
like a light switch
just before the light bulb is
blown the filament
broken torn apart.

Did your mother tell you things?
How she hated to iron
Pops shirts & crease his everyday
overalls over an ironing board
too heavy & luminously large
filling her small kitchen.

Did your father ever level
with you?
Tell you life's little secrets
kept secret from most people
except the few who
    are brave enough
    courageous enough
have the balls to
    expel it
    dispel it
    disarm it
of it's exploding powers—
to hear it and listen to it.

These are the keepers.
These are the keepers of the flame.

The torch is burning.
Burning hot & fiery
into our eyes
The fire glistening, lapping at our eyes

Mother,
It is before us.
Shall we take heed & carry forth the torch—
this Torch of Truth.
It will help us.
It will Light our way.

St. Matthew

i died on that fence.
i don't care what the medical
reports read.
my heart stopped beating then—
a proned, upright
Jesus Christ
with no vinegar to quench thirst.

"Hey... What's up? Do you mind if we sit here? I'm Aaron. This is Russell. Want another beer?"

they ripped me from the truck.
hair pulled in burning patches.
my face broken
again and again.
eyelids unable to open.
lips mauled
into pink fluid-like flesh and mush.

"We goin' your way. Wanta take a ride? See what kinda trouble we can get into?"

i tasted gunmetal,
although i was never shot.
the gun unloaded
against my skull.
numbness followed

by a red warm flow
descending cheeks.

"How's that feel, you cock sucker? This outta teach you about comin' on to another man. You fuckin' pervert."

they took my clothes.
ripped away shoes.
the chill cutting through
the overexposure.
i lay on the ground as
skies turned black.
i thought i felt the earth shake.
it was only me
throwing up blood and teeth.

"We saw how you was looking at our crotches."

i blacked out.
came to as hands hoisted
and tied.
splinters digging into
forearms.
i slobbered pleads.
cried blood for mercy.

"You go and tell all your fairy friends about what happens to fags. You hear?"

the sun faded as i did.
my body beaten, broken, barren,
and hung—
a welcome sign for tourists.

slowly inching toward
the death of life.

i watched unattached.
Life seeped from
what was left of me.
blood recycled in dirt.
a garden of flowers
where once hung
my carcass.

Splinters of Rejection

You walked in Palestine
Craters carved from your
Bones—
Mountains made with your
Tongue.
Your eyes burned with kindness
Too hot to touch
Too angelic to accept.

You stretched forth
Bloodied knuckles
    To hug the world
    To repair the world
    To divide the world
To cause a mother to be against her daughter,
A father to be against his son.
Your hands reached out for healing.
Miracles occurred at your fingertips.
You accepted lepers, prostitutes, homosexuals.
Your own said you had sinned.

Your voice sounded off like
Cannons
Exploding the eardrums
Of your constituents

Your profundity confounded them
Why would you share with such loathed few?
You had to be a hoax!
They railed you a madman.

The feet that would not give way
To water
Were the same that easily bled.
The hands that turned
Water to wine
Bound and defenseless.

You believed so greatly
What you lived that
You were willing to take the
Splinters of Rejection
For us all.

This Society

This Society has created in you the capacity to deny your very nature to make you long for normalcy while you bitterly pretend to be one of them.

This Society has enabled too many of Us to bury our feelings in a grave of shame hiding our faces in masks we neither want to need nor need to want.

This Society made it hard to be yourself Regal and Independent without shame and bitter aversion for the essence of your very basic nature your basic desires.

This Society fostered the detestation growing like fungus green and unyielding aided in the killings teaching our children to be afraid of Us to be ashamed of Us and themselves if they happen to be one of Us.

This Society laid waste the Pure Potentiality of Togetherness where all can stand and be counted and heard and respected.

Where all have a part a voice and a place in a Society that recognizes our differences as our Strength not our weakness.

Loving you was like a train wreck

poems of haiku and tanka

i remember you
with schizophrenic musings
the razor still cuts

i undulate you
still smelling your clothes and hair
the nightmare opens up

in the haze i scream
i see you with another
i do not trust snakes

i resist your calls
i cannot escape your breath
your face remains unwithered

you sit to cross me
lips moving but i don't hear
i can't feel my legs

my senses return
your tongue bleeding betrayal
my life now begins

i run through the swamps
alligators at my feet
vines tangling hair

when will the heart know
what the mind has come to know
lessons must be learned

you can't cut me now
i'm too far from the barbed wire
i mailed you the gauze

loving you was like
a train wreck frozen in time
your tongue the ice pick

true love does not hurt
so what have we really shared
hallucinations?

i sustain fragments
pieces of past existence
the stained glass shatters

the crickets invade
our bedroom like your penis
forcefully in me

the waterbed is
turbulent the tide sweeping
us outward with force
your thighs crushing my ribcage
pulling me under to drown

when i lost my mind
i thought it made you happy
you brought flowers as
i was having a seizure
you just sat there smiled and laughed

i dance in the field
the rain cool against my chest
i can laugh again

afterward i cried
washing your sex scent from me
a door between us

your words were violent
they had the power of life
used weapons of death

writing this frees me
unlocks the psychic wounding
i'm a dragonfly

Come forth and roll that Stone away

And when He thus had spoken, He cried with a loud voice, "Lazarus, come forth." And he that was dead came forth, bound hand and foot with grave clothes: and his face was bound with a napkin. Jesus saith unto them, 'Loose him, and let him go'."

—The Gospel According to Saint John 11:43-44

Conversation on Truth

i

The Truth

the Truth
while troublesome and
unbearable at times
lingers.

The echoes of
Freedom faint
Cannot be extinguished,
& like Jesus—
will not stay buried.

ii
The Preacher

the preacher said,
in his matter of fact voice,
that i had lied to
Everyone
that i was in fact a
fraud—
a judas dressed
in ceremonial robes.

but who's the liar?

how could i
lie about something
that he, in one of his Holy Ghost filled sermons,
said…
God could & would change
"Just surrender." His crooked fingers pointing in the direction
of my pew
"Just lay it on the altar."

but each time I surrendered
my knees hurt
and each time I knelt
i laid it out—
for the altar boys to take.

iii

Confession

what is it that
you
Fear?

the telling
the knowing
or the outcome of the telling?

spent lives
have been
wasted on
Fear.

Fear
is the illusion

for those whom it
mattered most,
soul down already know.

i am dead now

i am dead now.

my body, bones, and blood
ravished by this unrelenting virus
unremitting   took waste of my physical existence.

i don't even look like myself
a mere bag of bones
skin loosely hanging
about the purple casket lining.

my mother in her print dress
appreciating the flowers
and the turnout
worried aunts uncles surprised taken off guard
by this requiem showing.

they viewed my pillaged body and gossiped
whirlwinds around the room of rumors
unchecked and invalidated.

but i am dead now
and Free now
truly Free
finally Free

my mother cries
into a Kleenex and wails
why her baby—

she still tells the neighbors it was cancer.

Drag Queen

Work it girl
Don your eyelashes
Glue back your piece
Bobby pin your wig
Tight with style
Paint on your smile
For the world
To see.

Your breasts are gorgeous!
You don't even resemble
Yourself
You must be somebody else.

Caught between
A gendered world
girl or Boy
boy/Girl.

Pretending

i would have to peel my eyes away—
tearing them lid from lid
brand my skin—
preferably my forehead
eat my tongue
like a French delicacy
(words and all)
to help pretend this whole damn scene
is kosher.

moments of our love/real & imagined

i woke up beside you
the sun cutting through
shades like a
razor in flesh.
your dreadlocks
passionately flying
about your head like
a crown of thorns
you sleep in fits of
breath that rise and fall
as air escapes your mangoed lips—
i taste them
they are sweet and firm
and although not ripe
at the instant
ripen as you awaken.

the market is busy
with commerce
our eyes purvey the
antique glass and cabinets
painted chinese red.
the tea cups while oddly shaped
make a noted addition
to our collection

i twisted my ankle
on the cobble stoned streets
cars furiously rushing
by as we made our way
to the café of onlookers
smoking cigarettes and
downing coffee that could
walk itself.

we made love among
the mirrors
the jets cooled and
the glass fogged
the candles dripped
on the marble.

the taxi driver
took no notice
as your wet lips
descended.
however
i'm sure he heard
the moans.

you took me by
surprise
your shaft
engulfing enveloping
itself

you took my
hand and led me
across cattails
and water infested
with the larvae of
mosquitoes
spanish moss stuck
to our hair

i save clippings
of your fingernails
am careful to bag up your hair
afraid of losing
any part of you

my shaman
in dashiki
teach me the mysteries
show me the path

i lotion your
back—coconut oil
seeping in your pores
through the heat of
my fingers

you speak in tongues—
four languages
from your mouth
i taste them
on your lips

you seek to honor
the Truth
hold in esteem lessons
of the elders

you smile forth
another day—
the hands of time
hold still with your
breath.

you sail through
the room—
a cocktail in your
hand, your tony smile.

buddha smiles
in our window
as we sit cross legged
burning incense in our ashram.

your body gleams
from the flicker
of candlelight—
patchouli and lavender
rising from your skin

we ride horseback
bareback
through forests of pine
nakedly bridled and unfitted.

you explore me
deciphering cave paintings
etched
in my colon.

you left this
morning—a kiss
on my lips
i refuse to wash
before you return
your scent still lingers
on my fingertips

they tabooed us
before the gods
of the confederate
bbq in the pits
and bible tracks for
all to read.

we journeyed north
leaving roots and traditions
led by dreams of
stars and gold
holding onto
faith as small
as the seeds of mustard.

i taste your
cum like milk
your brown nipples
to suck from

Coming Out

Like Lazarus I came forth
Shedding the grave drapes of make believe
After hearing the voice of Authority say,
"Come Forth and Roll that stone away."
I etched my fate in man-made sand
That had, as long as I have had memory,
Been etched in stone.

This shroud had protected my shell
For so long that it stuck like
Melted band-aids,
And as I peeled it from me it took
Hair and layers of skin,
Leaving me wounded by a ditch in Jericho.

I was alone and awaited rescuing from
Friends I knew would soon pass-by
On their way home.
Instead, when they saw me naked
And honestly laid open, they quickly
Moved on with dirty rejection.
As they left I heard their comments.
Like:
"he deserves it, his nasty self."
And
"it just a'int natural."
And
"well, maybe he'll come to his senses if he suffers enough."

My situation quickly spread from
Jericho to Jerusalem and my parents
Came to see if they were telling the
Truth.
They viewed my body—
The wounds scabbing over slowly,
Slowly turning to scars

They asked if what the others had said was true.
I told them the Truth.
Then the Truth started hurting me again.
Their righteous indignation caused
Them to kick dirt in my face and infect
My now scabbing wounds.

My father said he was disgusted with me,
That he was ashamed and that I should also be ashamed.
He kicked me back into the ditch I have managed
To crawl from telling me to cover my nakedness.

He was afraid someone else may see me this way.
And make fun of him (god forbid)
For my "foolish, dirty deeds."

After a while they left—
My mother throwing up from fretting
My father—the veins in his neck
Bulging and pulsing with hatred red anger
His words still hung in the air like a thick fog.

It was at that moment:
Smelling my mother's rancid vomit
And rehearing the harsh cruel words of my father
That I realized I was alone.
Dirty Rejection.

I was alone in the same ditch.
My wounds now reopened and infected.
My Faith in the
Truth
shaken

Then it was at that moment I also realized
Jericho's night air and it's warming sun
Are machines for healing.
So for weeks I made love to the night air,
Received the warming cleansing sun,
Drank refreshing life giving waters from a nearby creek.
I ate berries that grew wildly and fancifully sweet.
All the while regaining my strength
For my journey home
To Jerusalem.

Within a while I fully recovered.
Now with new patches of hair—
Thicker, more shiny
And skin so thick that
It would defy the cutting of razors.

A Statue of Liberty?
(questions for the President)

Fairness. You talk of being fair?
Well, you ain't lived my life,
Worn my shoes, nor had my share.
Don't tell me of being fair.

Honest? You talk of living Truth?
Well, you ain't hungry,
And desperate enough to steal for food.
Don't tell me of being true.

Equal? You talk of Impartiality
When we can't adopt children
Because of our sexuality?
That ain't Equality.

Freedom? You tell me I'm free
When I can't be myself
And serve in your bloodied Army?
That shore ain't Liberty.

Our Love is a Forbidden Thing

No...you can't eat from that tree...they said with pointing fingers...the excuse...you may become too brilliant...too independent...adroit enough to think your own thoughts...own your own feelings...too possessed of knowledge...

But who can resist Ripe Fruit?...We were created for such delights...creatures with intestines...tongues that lap...bodies that crave...hands that freely roam...lips that suck...who can live without fruit?

So we partook...eating like greedy gods...chins dripping...sugared sweet...afterwards...we wiped our chins...clean from sin...it was our sticky fingers...cotton candied hands...that gave us away...

We were cast out of Eden...by our creators...the charges were as follows...Civil Disobedience...they asked if we...would like to say something...in our defense...

Our only reply...and rebuttal...
Who can live without fruit?

Pride March

The guy at the Pride March
asked me, as rainbow colored floats paraded by,
"So...are you straight? Or Bi? Or just plain out gay?"

i looked him over,
his bleached blonde hair gi styled,
tattoos descending his torso,
tan lined buttocks hanging from his chaps, and replied,
"I'm Human."

We are all the Same

We have crouched too long
In unlighted streets
Living the Calamity of our
Discretions.
We have quietly heaved
The guilt you've
Placed upon us.
Your congressmen, Senators, Lawmakers
Making laws to
Protect you
From us.

But we have a simple
Being—
To love and be loved
In the open.
Able to walk hand in hand
Without utterances of disapproval.
To be regarded with
Simple dignity and rights
That belong not to an individual people
But to everyone.
Gay & Straight
Straight & Gay
We are all the Same.
We are all the Same.

Extend to Us
The same protections that protect
And secure your families.
Our family is waiting with
Anguished slaughtered martyrs
From Stonewall to Matthew Shepard
History is writing itself.
We must retaliate.
We have lived in the darkness
For far too long.
It's time to stand and hold our ground.
It's time to scream and yell and cry
Our rights cannot be denied!
Our voices will not be extinguished.
It's time to fight
For the Freedom of simply
Being.

It's the ignorance
That has forced us
To the levels of bathhouses.
It's the ignorance
That causes a mother to
Spit in her daughters face.
It's the ignorance
That causes fathers to
Bash in our skulls
And deny our very existence.
It's the ignorance
That gives churches the right
To morality

That judges everyone according
To their own belief.
It's the ignorance
That has caused us to lose our homes, our jobs,
Our very lives.
It's the ignorance
That has forced us to pretend
Leaving too many more hurt people.

We have lingered too long.
We have crouched too low.
This unrelenting blackness must cease.
This unending terror must end.
We must come together.
Because
We are all the Same.
Gay & Straight
Straight & Gay
We are all the Same.

Our being is simple.
To love and be loved
In the open daylight
Walking freely—
Hand in hand
Gay & Straight
Straight & Gay
We are all the Same.
We are all the Same.

For information regarding speaking engagements or readings
Contact:
Jeanine Grande Wilson at
grandejean@aol.com

0-595-27071-9

Printed in the United States
41678LVS00005B/295

9 780595 270712